W9-BIN-312

RAINBOW
CRAFTS

Andra Serlin Abramson

STERLING INNOVATION

An imprint of Sterling Publishing Co., Inc.

New York / London
www.sterlingpublishing.com

STERLING and the distinctive Sterling logo are
registered trademarks of
Sterling Publishing Co., Inc.

2 4 6 8 10 9 7 5 3 1

Published by Sterling Publishing Co., Inc.
387 Park Avenue South, New York, NY 10016
© 2008 by Sterling Publishing Co., Inc.

Distributed in Canada by Sterling Publishing
c/o Canadian Manda Group, 165 Dufferin Street
Toronto, Ontario, Canada M6K 3H6
Distributed in the United Kingdom by GMC Distribution Services
Castle Place, 166 High Street, Lewes, East Sussex, England BN7 1XU
Distributed in Australia by Capricorn Link (Australia) Pty. Ltd.
P.O. Box 704, Windsor, NSW 2756, Australia

Printed in China
All rights reserved

Sterling ISBN-13: 978-1-4027-5727-3
ISBN-10: 1-4027-5727-1

For information about custom editions, special sales, premium and
corporate purchases, please contact Sterling Special Sales
Department at 800-805-5489 or specialsales@sterlingpublishing.com.

Illustrations by Julia Rothman

CONTENTS

INTRODUCTION

QUESTION: What can you make with craft sticks and chenille sticks?

ANSWER: A lot of cool crafts. Chenille sticks and craft sticks are among the most versatile craft ingredients out there. As you'll see from the wide range of projects found in this book, you'll be able to bend, cut, glue, and make these simple materials into outrageous and imaginative crafts to liven up any space or bring a smile to anyone's face. Plus, these crafts are easy to do and don't take a lot of time.

Here are a few basic hints to help you before you get started:

1. Use a good pair of scissors to cut craft sticks to the right length. Safety scissors won't work for this. An adult will need to help you with the cutting.

2. When using chenille sticks, you often will need to ask an adult to help you use a glue gun to make sure the chenille stick really sticks. Regular craft glue will work for some materials (gluing tissue paper to the chenille stick, for example) but if you try regular glue and it doesn't work immediately, it probably won't hold even once it dries.

3. If any instructions don't seem clear, check the picture. They say that "a picture is worth a thousand words," so looking at what the finished craft will look like is a good way to help interpret the directions.

4. Use your imagination. Look for ways to improve and expand these crafts. Make something new and unique that only you could have created.

5. Check out your local craft store. Many craft materials and decorations are super cheap and can add a touch of pizzazz to any project.

So don't just sit there—gather together your materials, and let's get crafty!

FANCY FLOWERPOTS

Don't have a green thumb? Doesn't matter! Just use your craft materials to jazz up those boring clay flowerpots. You may find that the pot becomes prettier than the flowers you grow in it.

WHAT YOU NEED

clay flowerpot
craft sticks
glue gun
chenille sticks
other craft materials
(as desired)

LET'S GET CRAFTY

1. Measure the distance from the bottom of the flowerpot to the point where the edge juts out.

2. Cut a bunch of craft sticks to this length and glue them side-by-side to the pot all the way around. Because the pot is wider at the top than it is at the bottom, the sticks will start to slant to one side. Once the sticks get very slanted, start gluing the sticks in the other direction, leaving a V shape between the sticks. Or use smaller craft sticks to fill in the extra space so the whole clay pot is covered.

3. Cut some additional craft sticks or use other craft materials to decorate the pot. Try using geometric patterns and designs. You might even try making letters or words, or shapes such as hearts. Don't forget to put something into those V-shaped spaces.

4. Using a glue gun, glue chenille sticks and other decorations all around the top edge of the pot. Make it colorful!

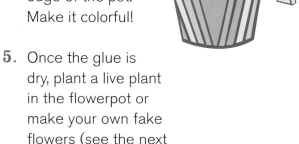

5. Once the glue is dry, plant a live plant in the flowerpot or make your own fake flowers (see the next page) to spruce up any room.

FLOWERS, FLOWERS, EVERYWHERE

Once your flowerpot is done, make your own flowers to put in it. These flowers will brighten up any room and will never wilt or need watering.

WHAT YOU NEED

chenille sticks
pom-pom balls
glue gun
a block of florist's foam
scissors

LET'S GET CRAFTY

1. Gather a few chenille sticks and bend them into basic flower shapes. Twist the ends together in the center of the flower to hold the shape together.

2. Use one more chenille stick to make a long stem for the flower and twist one end around the center of the flower. The other end will stick into the flowerpot.

3. Glue a pom-pom ball to the center of the flower.

4. Cut the florist's foam to fit into your flowerpot. Stick the stems of the flowers into the foam. Viola! Flowers for everyone!

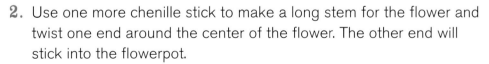

YOU'RE SO ADVANCED!

Want to go one step further? Find some tissue paper and glue to try this.

1. Before putting the pom-pom ball in the center of the flower, place glue all around one side of the flower shape (but not the stem part).

2. Place the flower glue-side down on a piece of colored tissue paper.

3. When the glue is dry, cut off the excess paper so that only the flower shape remains.

4. Glue the pom-pom to the center of the flower and then decorate the tissue paper, if you'd like.

TRAVEL TIC-TAC-TOE

Heading out of town? Running to catch the bus? Now you can take your favorite game on the road with this simple and fun craft.

WHAT YOU NEED

craft sticks
glue
chenille sticks
scissors

LET'S GET CRAFTY

1. Place enough craft sticks side-by-side to make a square shape.

2. Place two craft sticks horizontally across the square and two craft sticks vertically on the square to form the shape of a typical tic-tac-toe board.

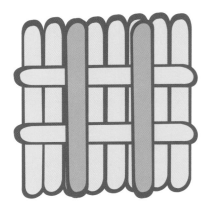

3. Glue these down, making sure that the bottom two craft sticks lie lengthwise across the square, touching all the craft sticks to hold the bottom of the board together.

4. Cut a chenille stick in half and coil it into a one-inch circle. This is an O. Make five of these.

5. Cut a different-color chenille stick into thirds. Twist or glue two of the pieces together into an X shape. Make five of these.

6. Find a partner and play!

YOU'RE SO ADVANCED!

Make a little bag to hold your travel game so you can always find the pieces. All you'll need is some scrap fabric (or try an old kitchen towel or pillowcase), string, and a glue gun.

1. Cut two squares of fabric about one inch (2.5 cm) bigger on all sides than your tic-tac-toe board.

2. Glue the bottom of the two pieces of fabric together.

3. Glue about three-fourths of the two sides together. Don't glue all the way to the top.

4. Place one end of the string on the fabric at the top of the bag and fold the fabric over it. Make sure the end of the string remains outside of the bag. Glue the fabric down over the string to create a drawstring top. Do the same with the other side of the bag so that the string is completely covered.

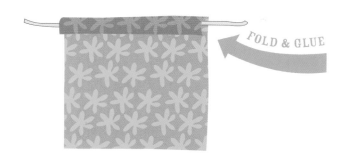

FOLD & GLUE

5. Tie the ends of the string together.

6. Finish gluing the sides together.

7. When the glue is dry, turn the bag inside out so you can't see the glue lines.

8. Place your tic-tac-toe board and the playing pieces into the bag, pull shut, and go.

BIRDSONG HOUSES

Birds make beautiful music for us. Now you can share your favorite music with the birds by making a birdsong house. Add birdseed and it becomes a bird feeder. The birds will thank you for it.

WHAT YOU NEED

craft sticks
glue gun
a small box bottom
  (a milk carton with the
  top cut off will work well)
thick string or yarn
lyrics from your favorite song
scissors
acrylic clear coat

LET'S GET CRAFTY

1. Glue craft sticks all the way around three sides of the box to make the walls.

2. Lay out the last wall as above, but this time don't glue it. First, sketch a circular opening on the craft sticks that the birds will use as their window to enter and exit the birdhouse. Shade in this circle.

3. Pick up each individual craft stick and cut out the shaded region with your scissors. Put the sticks back into place and glue a horizontal stick across the top and bottom to hold the sticks in place. Remember not to block the window.

13

4. Glue the sticks to the box as you did in the first step to make the fourth wall. If necessary, cut the hole in the box wall as well.

5. To make the roof, lay three craft sticks in a triangular shape so that the edges of the sticks overlap.

6. Lay craft sticks across the triangle along the left edge so that they overlap the right edge. Use scissors to trim off the edges of the sticks on the right side to make a triangle. Save your extra pieces, you'll use them to make a second triangle.

7. Glue the three triangular sticks to the craft sticks to hold the triangle shape in place. Repeat steps 5, 6, and 7 to make a second triangle.

8. Add a few extra craft sticks around the edges of the triangles to give them more surface area. This will make it easier to glue.

9. Lay craft sticks in a square shape and glue three craft sticks across them at the top, middle, and bottom to hold them in place. Repeat to make a second square.

10. Lay the squares against the triangles to make a pitched roof. Use the glue gun to glue the pieces together to complete the roof. There will be space between the two sides of the roof.

11. Punch a small hole though the bottom of the birdhouse and thread thick rope or yarn though the hole. Tie a big knot in the rope under the bottom of the birdhouse to keep the rope in place.

12. Thread the rope through the top of the birdhouse so you can hang it.

13. Decorate with a printout of the lyrics of your favorite song and glue them in random or orderly patterns, depending on your style. Add the song title in permanent marker. Add pictures, if you'd like.

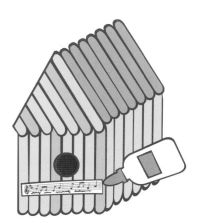

14. Paint on acrylic clear coat and let dry. This will seal your lyrics.

15. Buy some birdseed if you want to feed the birds.

YOU'RE SO ADVANCED!

Add a bit of flair to your birdhouse with these extra features:

• Give the birds a place to perch when entering your birdhouse by gluing small pieces of craft sticks together and then gluing these to the outside of the birdhouse just under the window.

• To keep the squirrels away from the bird feeder, get a large piece of plastic (one of those plastic saucers that goes under plants to keep the water from going everywhere works well), carefully cut a hole in the middle, and place it above the roof of the birdhouse by threading the string through it. This keeps the squirrels from landing on the birdhouse from above and getting to the food.

MARDI GRAS MASK

When Mardi Gras rolls around, it's time to party New Orleans Style. But what should you wear? How about your very own personally-designed Mardi Gras mask?

WHAT YOU NEED

craft sticks
cardboard
glue
scissors
sequins
feathers
chenille sticks
a long dowel

LET'S GET CRAFTY

1. Before you begin, you might want to sketch a design of what you would like your mask to look like.

2. Lay out your craft sticks on a piece of cardboard in the shape you'd like and decide where your eyes will go.

3. Draw large ovals on the craft sticks where you want the eyes and shade them in.

4. One by one, remove each piece that is shaded and cut the shaded portion out. Replace the sticks where they should go and trace the eye holes on the cardboard beneath the sticks.

5. Carefully remove the cardboard and cut the eyeholes out. Replace the sticks on the cardboard and glue them down.

6. Accentuate your theme. Add sequins, feathers, chenille sticks, or anything else you need to add to your design.

7. Glue a dowel (a long, thin piece of wood or other material) to the back of the mask. Hold the mask by the part of the dowel that hangs down below the bottom of the mask. Now you have an easy way to hold the mask up to maintain your secret identity.

8. Let the party begin.

PERFECT PENCIL HOLDER

Never a pen or a pencil around when you need it? Solve that problem with style by making this picture perfect pencil holder. Then every time you reach for a pencil you'll think, "I made this!"

WHAT YOU NEED

a can without any sharp edges
   (a peanut can, a frozen orange
   juice carton, or any cylindrical
   shape that you can work with)
craft sticks
glue
chenille sticks
other craft supplies

LET'S GET CRAFTY

1. Select a pattern of colors and glue your colored sticks to the can in that pattern. It's OK if the sticks are longer than the can. Depending on the diameter of the can, you may need to adjust the width of the last craft stick to make it fit.

2. Once the glue is dry, tie chenille sticks around the can. Use as many chenille sticks as you like. Twist the edges of the chenille sticks into fun shapes.

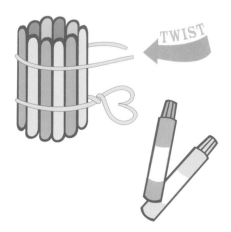

3. Decorate the rest of the can with craft materials or markers.

Celebrate Flag Day, the Fourth of July, or just be patriotic with this super flag pencil holder:

1. Glue red and white craft sticks three-fourths of the way around your can.

2. Cut blue craft sticks into thirds and glue them horizontally the remainder of the way around the can.

3. When the glue is dry, glue white star shapes (foam works well) to the blue portion of the can.

4. Say the Pledge of Allegiance.

BEAUTIFUL, BEAUTIFUL BUTTERFLY

Butterflies always brighten up the summer. Now you can invite these beautiful creatures inside no matter what time of the year it is. Make a bunch of these to hang in the corner of your room, and you'll always feel like it's nice outside.

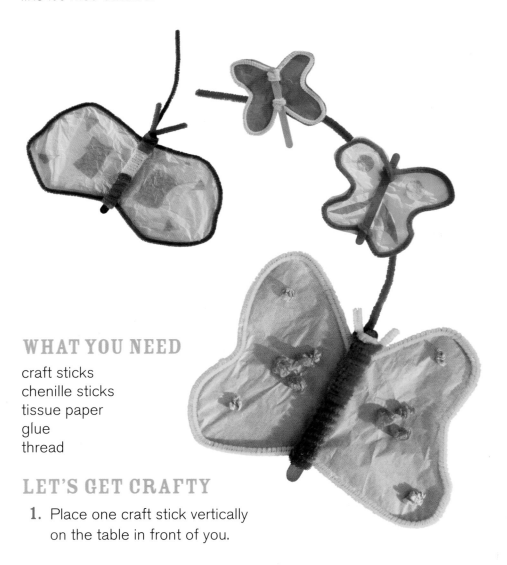

WHAT YOU NEED

craft sticks
chenille sticks
tissue paper
glue
thread

LET'S GET CRAFTY

1. Place one craft stick vertically on the table in front of you.

2. Bend a chenille stick to make antennae. Place the bent part of the chenille stick on the craft stick and wrap the craft stick with more chenille sticks to form the body.

WRAP

3. Bend two chenille sticks to make wing shapes.

4. Glue or twist the ends of the chenille stick wings to the craft stick.

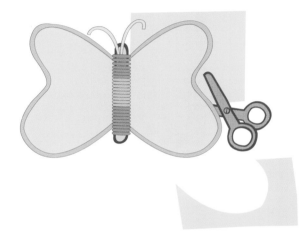

5. Place the butterfly shape on a piece of tissue paper. Glue the edges of the wings to the tissue paper. After it dries, cut the excess paper from around the chenille frame.

6. Mix a small amount of glue with some water to make the glue a little watery. This will keep the glue from soaking through the tissue paper. Using the diluted glue, add colored stripes or dots of tissue paper to the wings on both sides and allow to dry.

7. When you are done, tie about eighteen inches (45 cm) of thread to the top of the butterfly frame, then hang the butterflies by a window or in your room.

YOU'RE SO ADVANCED!

Don't just stop at butterflies. Add to the menagerie by making dragonflies, birds, clouds, even airplanes.

A CRAFTY PHOTO FRAME

Place your favorite vacation photos in a frame you make yourself. Vary the theme of the frame to whatever type of vacation you took. Use a woods theme for camping, ticket stubs and park logos from an amusement park vacation, or even fake snow for a ski trip.

WHAT YOU NEED

an inexpensive plastic photo frame
a small photograph
craft sticks
glue
other craft materials or souvenirs from your trip

LET'S GET CRAFTY

1. Glue the craft sticks around the edge of the frame, making sure you leave enough room to see your photo. Insert your photo and think about what theme you'd like to use.

2. Dig up souvenirs from your trip or gather craft materials to enhance the frame. Small wooden painted shapes from the craft store are inexpensive and are a great way to liven up your frame.

3. Do it again! This one is so fun you'll want to decorate all your photo frames.

Make an ordinary frame into something extraordinary by creating a shape that fits with your photo. For example, if your photo is of you and your brother playing football, create a football-shaped frame to go with it. For a trip to the zoo, you could add a long neck like a giraffe. For a graduation photo, make the frame in the shape of those funny graduation hats.

WOVEN CHENILLE STICK COASTERS

If you've ever made woven pot holders, you already know how to do this. Just remember it's "Over then Under, then it's Under then Over." No problem!

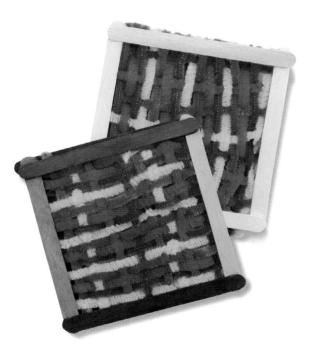

WHAT YOU NEED

craft sticks
glue gun
chenille sticks
scissors

LET'S GET CRAFTY

1. Place four craft sticks in a square shape so that the tips overlap. Glue the tips together and let the glue dry.

2. Glue the edges of eight chenille sticks to one side of the square. These are the pieces you will be weaving around.

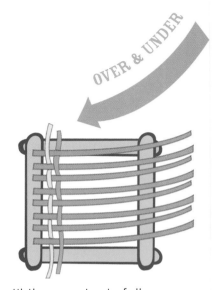

OVER & UNDER

3. Starting from one of the sides, use a chenille stick to weave over and under the chenille sticks you glued down. Push each stick to the top once you are done weaving it. Make them tight against each other. Repeat until the coaster is full.

4. When you are finished weaving, trim the excess chenille sticks all the way around the square.

5. Glue four craft sticks to the top edges of the coaster to sandwich the ends of the chenille sticks and to give the coaster more durability.

6. You might want to make a few of these. They'll come in handy!

CRAFT STICK KITE MAGNET

Nobody likes an unadorned refrigerator. Create this fun kite magnet to put an end to those boring fridge blues.

WHAT YOU NEED

craft sticks
glue
ribbon
chenille stick
magnet backing
foam letters or markers

LET'S GET CRAFTY

1. Arrange the craft sticks of many colors into a diamond shape. (This is the same as a square shape, but slightly tilted.)

2. Draw glue lines around the outer edges of the diamond shape and place craft sticks on the glue to hold the whole thing together.

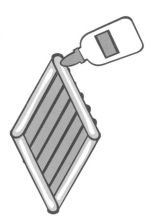

3. Glue a piece of ribbon to the back of the diamond and cut to the right length for a tail.

4. Make bow shapes out of chenille sticks and tie them to the tail.

5. Glue a magnet to the back. Make sure the magnet is strong enough to support your kite.

6. Turn the kite over and put a message on the front of your kite.

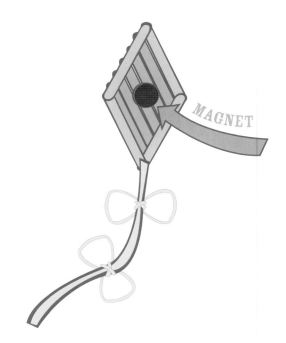

YOU'RE SO ADVANCED

Kites not your thing? Make a different shape for your magnet or even celebrate your favorite holiday with a themed magnet. Try a picket fence with flowers growing over it for Mother's Day, a heart shape for Valentine's, or a tie-shape for your dad. Let your imagination go, and soon your fridge will be the snazziest one on the block.

SUPER SHADOWBOX

Display your favorite little treasures in this super little shadowbox.
A bunch of these hung together on a wall look really, well, super.

WHAT YOU NEED

craft sticks
glue
your favorite little treasures

LET'S GET CRAFTY

1. Lay out four craft sticks so that they form a square, with their ends overlapping. Glue the ends together.

2. Continue adding craft sticks until the shadow box is as deep as you need it to be.

3. Lay craft sticks side-by-side so that they form a square. Glue three craft sticks horizontally at the top, middle, and bottom of the square to hold it together.

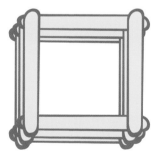

4. Glue this piece to the bottom of your shadowbox to form the back.

5. Set your treasures inside the shadowbox, then hang it on a wall to display them.

WONDERFUL WIND CHIMES

You and the wind can make beautiful music together with this simple but elegant wind chime. If you plan on hanging this outside where it can get wet, make sure you use waterproof material. Otherwise, try hanging it just inside a window or door to keep it safe and dry.

WHAT YOU NEED

a small clay flowerpot
chenille sticks
glue gun
craft materials
string
some kind of noisemaker
 (bells work well)

LET'S GET CRAFTY

1. Using a glue gun (it won't work without one), glue chenille sticks around the entire body of the pot.

2. Decorate the top edge of the pot with whatever you'd like. You could use beads, pieces of sea glass, rocks, even pom-poms (but remember, it will be hanging upside down).

3. Attach string to your noisemakers. Make them all different lengths.

4. Glue the edges of the string to the inside of the pot at what would normally be the top.

5. Cut a long piece of string and make a big knot in one end.

6. Push the other end of the string through the bottom of the pot, where the water would normally drain.

7. Grab the end of the string and make sure the knot you tied will hold on the inside of the pot.

8. Hang in a place with some wind. Ah, what beautiful music you've made.

KNOT

A GREETING CARD THEY WON'T THROW AWAY

If sending a greeting card shows you like someone, making your own card really shows where the love is. This greeting card is so awesome there is no way the recipient will throw it away.

WHAT YOU NEED

craft sticks
glue
cardboard
foam letters
markers
googly eyes
craft sticks
other craft materials

1. Lay out your craft sticks in a square shape. Glue one craft stick horizontally across the top of the sticks, and one craft stick horizontally across the bottom to hold the shape together. This is the front of your card.

2. Repeat step 1 to make the back of your card.

1/2"

4"

3. Find a piece of cardboard that has a natural crease in it (if possible), such as the connected top and side of a box. Cut the cardboard so that it is about four inches (10 cm) tall by about one-and-a-half inches (4 cm) wide, with about one-half inch (1.5 cm) of cardboard on either side of the crease. This piece will make the card open and close properly.

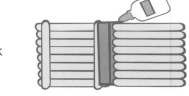

4. Glue one side of the crease to the back of the front panel of the card, and the other side of the crease to the back of the back panel. The card should open and close easily.

5. Decorate the card for whatever holiday, event, or greeting you'd like. If you plan on sending the card through the mail, remember to wrap it carefully and add the correct postage.

THE CRISS-CROSS BOX

Put your favorite jewelry or treasures in this fancy box. With peek-a-boo holes in the top, you won't even have to open it to see what's inside.

WHAT YOU NEED

a small cardboard box with a top
  (about 4 inches or 10 cm square, like a watch box)
craft sticks
glue
scissors
other craft materials as desired

LET'S GET CRAFTY

1. Remove the box top and draw a line about one-half inch (1.5 cm) in from the top edge all the way around.

2. Cut along the line with the scissors and remove the cardboard piece.

TRIM

3. Lay craft sticks across the box top in a slanted pattern so that they lay on the one-half-inch (1.5 cm) ledge. Cut the craft sticks to fit from corner to corner and then glue them down.

4. Repeat step 3 but lay the craft sticks in the opposite direction to create a criss-cross effect.

5. Replace the box top.

6. Use craft sticks or other craft materials to decorate the rest of the box as you like.

YOU'RE SO ADVANCED!

Ever try mosaics? To give it a try here, cut a bunch of craft sticks into small pieces with different angles. Glue the small pieces very close to each other in a random pattern all the way around the bottom of the box (remember not to cover the part where the box top fits). Fill in the spaces between the pieces of craft sticks with white glue, being careful to wipe off the excess glue off the craft sticks before it dries.

BEADED FRIENDSHIP BRACELETS

Make bracelets and anklets to go with every one of your outfits (and every one of your friends' outfits) with this simple beaded craft.

WHAT YOU NEED

chenille sticks
beads

LET'S GET CRAFTY

1. Cut a chenille stick to fit around your wrist or ankle, leaving a little bit extra to twist closed.

2. Find beads with holes large enough for the chenille stick to fit through.

3. Bead 'till you drop.

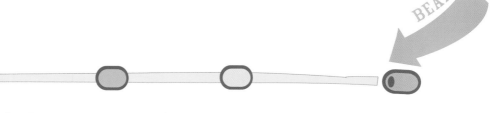

BEAD

4. Twist the two ends of the chenille sticks together to close the bracelet and keep the beads in place.

Find some small safety pins and make this cool beaded anklet.

1. Open the safety pin and carefully bead some small beads onto the sharp prong. Make sure you can still close the safety pin completely. Repeat until you have all the beaded pins you need.

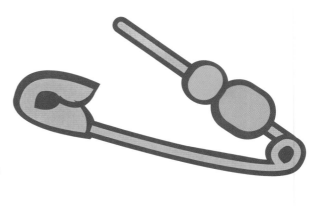

2. String the beaded safety pins onto a chenille stick cut to the right length for your ankle.

3. Place other small beads in between each safety pin to keep the pins apart and allow them to hang properly.

4. Wear all summer long.

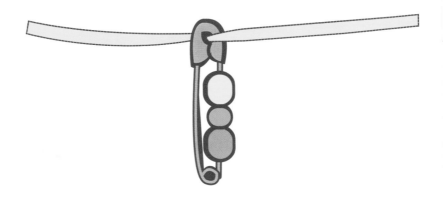

SCHOOL COLORS HAIR CLIP

Even if you're not on the pep squad, you can still show your support for your school by making and wearing a hairclip in your school colors.

WHAT YOU NEED

chenille sticks
hairclip of some kind
ribbon
glue
beads
your school's initials in foam letter stickers

LET'S GET CRAFTY

1. Pick out chenille sticks in your school's colors.

2. Wrap the top of the hairclip (but not the part that closes it) with chenille sticks. You can choose to wrap one color halfway and then use the other color, or you can alternate the colors.

3. Trim off any extra chenille stick ends.

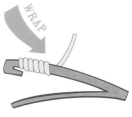

4. Glue some ribbon to the hairclip. Add beads to the end of the ribbon, if you'd like.

5. Peel off the tape backing and attach your school's initials to the chenille-wrapped hairclip (for example, if you went to Westbury High School, you could attach a "W" and an "H" or "WHS").

6. Wear with pride.

YOU'RE SO ADVANCED!

Not enough hair for a hairclip? You can still show your support by making a school color pin. Just follow the directions above, but use a pin instead of a hairclip.

CRAZY PROPELLER HAT AND FAIRY HEADBAND

Even if it isn't Halloween, you can still have a little fun with these crazy hats. Feel free to add your own embellishments to the designs. When you use your imagination, you never know what you might come up with.

WHAT YOU NEED

chenille sticks
craft flowers
ribbon

LET'S GET CRAFTY

CRAZY PROPELLER HAT

1. Twist one end of two chenille sticks together. Measure around your head and twist the other two ends together at the right length to fit.

2. Twist the end of another chenille stick to the circle you made. Twist the other end of this chenille stick to the opposite side of the circle. Bend the chenille stick into an arch.

3. Repeat step 2 three or four times to shape the hat.

4. Make propellers by twisting the middle of a chenille stick or two around the chenille sticks where they cross in the center of the hat, and then bending the ends into a propeller shape.

FAIRY HEADBAND

1. Twist one end of two chenille sticks together. Measure around your head and twist the other two ends together at the right length to fit.

2. Twist the stems of some craft flowers around the front of the headband. Make sure the flowers are close together so that you get a full effect. The flowers should start above one ear and end above the other.

3. Tie long pieces of ribbon to the back of the headband for a flowing, romantic effect.

MIRROR, MIRROR ON THE WALL

Make a mirror that will never talk back (unless it is to say how fabulous you are) with the craft materials found in this kit (and any other cool decorations you have lying around, just waiting to be used).

WHAT YOU NEED

craft sticks
glue gun
a small mirror
chenille sticks
beads or other craft materials

1. Lay a bunch of craft sticks side-by-side. Make sure the craft sticks are longer than width of the mirror.

2. Glue two or three craft sticks cross-wise to hold the rows of craft sticks together. Once the glue dries, flip the craft stick board over.

3. Place the mirror in the center of the craft stick board and glue down.

4. Glue chenille sticks around the edges of the mirror. Add decorations to the sides of the mirror, but remember to leave enough room to be able to see your face.

5. Glue a chenille stick to the back of the mirror for hanging.

FRIENDS FOREVER MESSAGE BOARD

Make a special gift for your best friend with this crafty message board. This project is also great for making door signs and locker decorations.

WHAT YOU NEED

craft sticks
glue
a chenille stick
foam letters or markers

1. Lay the craft sticks side-by-side in whatever pattern you like. Make sure you make the board long enough for whatever message you want to put on it.

2. Glue additional craft sticks horizontally across the board to hold the vertical sticks in place. Use as many sticks as you need to depending on the size of your message board. Let the glue dry.

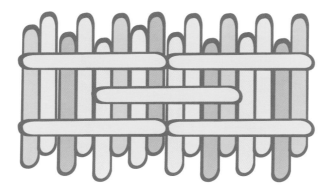

3. Cut a chenille stick in half and glue each end to the back of the message board. This will be the hanger.

4. Flip the message board over and add your message. From "Friends Forever" to "Be My Valentine," you'll really get your point across with this craft.

Take this craft to the next level by adding some extra crafty elements. Have ribbon hanging from the bottom, add glitter or sparkly paint, or use beads or feathers to enhance your message.

RING TOSS FOR EVERYONE

Ring toss is the perfect game. Just when it seems like it is getting easier you can take a step backward and make it hard again. And everyone, from young to old, can complete on the same level. So let's get going and make our own ring toss game.

WHAT YOU NEED

craft sticks
glue
chenille sticks
paper
pencil

1. Glue four craft sticks together, one on top of the other, then glue a craft stick flat to each side of the craft stick pile. This will be the ring toss pin.

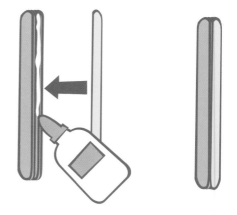

2. Lay eleven craft sticks side-by-side. Remove the middle stick so that there are only ten sticks with a hole in the middle.

3. Glue four craft sticks horizontally across the ten craft sticks (leaving the space where the eleventh one used to be) so that there is one craft stick at the top, one at the bottom, and two in the middle. The middle two should be one craft-stick-width apart. This is the base of the ring toss game.

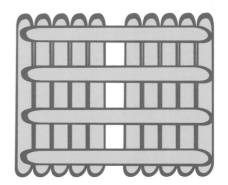

4. Before the glue on the base dries completely, stick the ring toss pin into the center of the hole in the base. Adjust the horizontal craft sticks to make it fit if necessary.

5. To keep the pin steady, glue two craft sticks flat on top of the two horizontal craft sticks that are holding the pin. Then glue two craft sticks flat on the two other sides of the pin. Repeat three or four times, until the pin is held firmly in place. Let the glue dry.

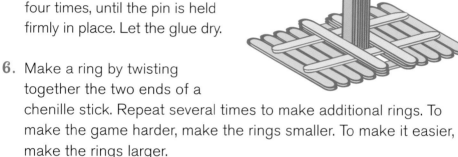

6. Make a ring by twisting together the two ends of a chenille stick. Repeat several times to make additional rings. To make the game harder, make the rings smaller. To make it easier, make the rings larger.

7. To play this game, make three or four ring toss pins and four rings in the same color for each person. Place the pins at different distances from where you will be throwing, and assign points for each pin based on how far away the pin is. Have each person throw his or her rings and use paper and pencil to keep track of everyone's point total.

PRETTY BRAIDED BRACELETS

This pretty bracelet is super-easy to make. Don't just make one. Your friends will love them as much as you do. Plus, they look great in lots of different colors.

WHAT YOU NEED

three chenille sticks
pretty ribbon
glue

LET'S GET CRAFTY

1. Twist one end of three chenille sticks together.

2. Braid the three craft sticks together just like you were braiding your hair.

3. When the braid is long enough to slip over your hand, twist the ends of the braid together and cut off the extra length of the chenille sticks.

4. Twist the two ends of the bracelet together to form a circle.

5. Wrap a small piece of ribbon around the twisted ends and glue it in place. This is to make sure the ends don't poke you.

6. Loosely wrap the rest of your ribbon around the bracelet and tie the ends with a bow.

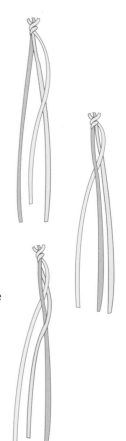

YOU'RE SO ADVANCED!

Make it a charm bracelet! With permission, raid your mom's inexpensive jewelry box, or your own junk drawer for some small unused charms. Use pieces of ribbon to attach the charms to your bracelet. Make sure you tie them on tightly so you don't lose them. Look for charms that express who you are. If you like horses, try and find a horse charm. If you're into music, look for musical notes.

LET'S GET CRAFTY